CHILDREN'S STORYTELLERS

Maurice Sendak

by Chris Bowman

BELLWETHER MEDIA • MINNEAPOLIS, MN

Note to Librarians, Teachers, and Parents:

Blastoff! Readers are carefully developed by literacy experts and combine standards-based content with developmentally appropriate text.

Level 1 provides the most support through repetition of high-frequency words, light text, predictable sentence patterns, and strong visual support.

Level 2 offers early readers a bit more challenge through varied simple sentences, increased text load, and less repetition of high-frequency words.

Level 3 advances early-fluent readers toward fluency through increased text and concept load, less reliance on visuals, longer sentences, and more literary language.

Level 4 builds reading stamina by providing more text per page, increased use of punctuation, greater variation in sentence patterns, and increasingly challenging vocabulary.

Level 5 encourages children to move from "learning to read" to "reading to learn" by providing even more text, varied writing styles, and less familiar topics.

Whichever book is right for your reader, Blastoff! Readers are the perfect books to build confidence and encourage a love of reading that will last a lifetime!

This edition first published in 2016 by Bellwether Media, Inc.

Library of Congress Cataloging-in-Publication Data

Bowman, Chris, 1990-
Maurice Sendak / by Chris Bowman.
pages cm. – (Blastoff! Readers: Children's Storytellers)
Summary: "Simple text and full-color photographs introduce readers to Maurice Sendak. Developed by literacy experts for students in second through fifth grade"– Provided by publisher.
Includes bibliographical references and index.
ISBN 978-1-62617-341-5 (hardcover : alk. paper)
1. Sendak, Maurice–Juvenile literature. 2. Authors, American–20th century–Biography–Juvenile literature. 3. Children's literature–Authorship–Juvenile literature. 4. Illustrators–United States–Biography–Juvenile literature. I. Title.
PS3569.E6Z56 2016
813'.54–dc23
[B]
2015030693

Printed in the United States of America, North Mankato, MN.

Table of Contents

Who Was Maurice Sendak?

Maurice Sendak was a beloved children's author and **illustrator**. Throughout his life, Maurice illustrated almost 100 picture books, including 20 that he wrote.

Maurice changed the idea that children's books must always be **innocent**. His books were known for their imaginative and sometimes scary pictures. These drawings earned him a **Caldecott Medal** in 1964 for one book, *Where the Wild Things Are*.

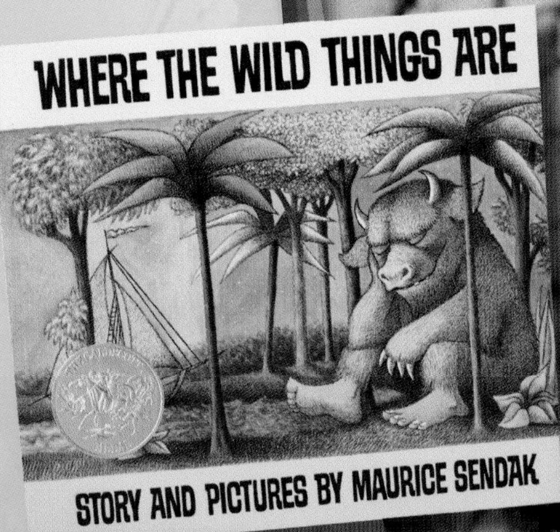

In Bed by Day

Maurice Sendak was born on June 10, 1928. He grew up in Brooklyn, New York, with his older siblings, Jack and Natalie.

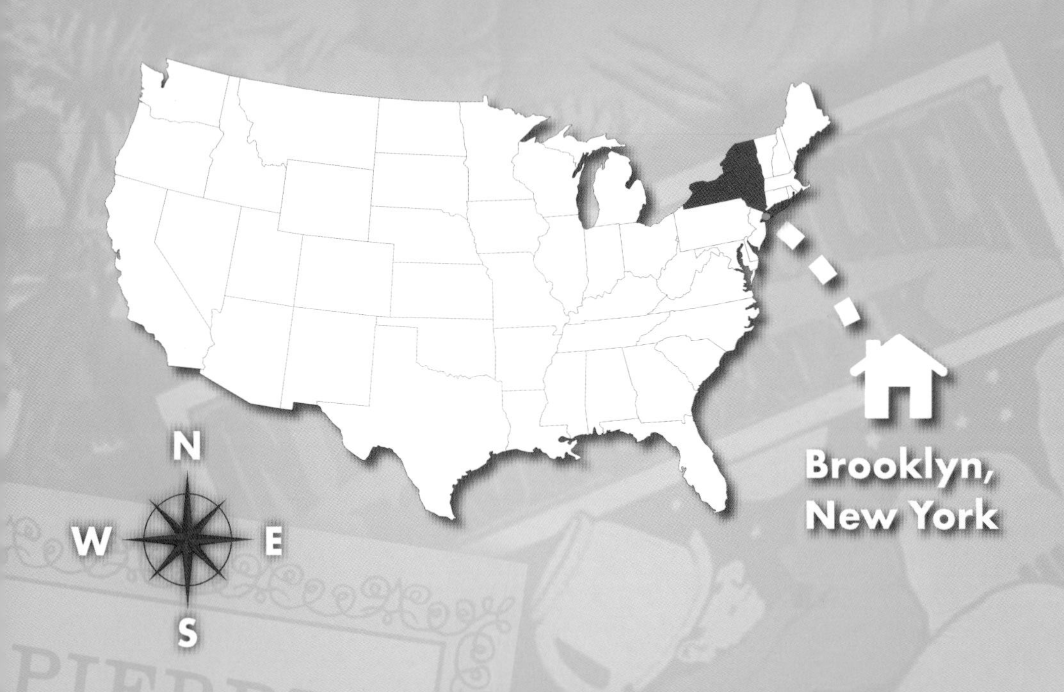

"No story is worth the writing, no picture is worth the making, if it is not a work of the imagination."
Maurice Sendak

fun fact

Maurice liked classical music. His favorite composer was Mozart.

When he was young, Maurice was often sick. He spent a lot of time in bed looking out his window. Maurice drew what he could see. Then his brother wrote stories about the pictures.

"Grown-ups always say they protect their children, but they're really protecting themselves. Besides, you can't protect children. They know everything."

Maurice Sendak

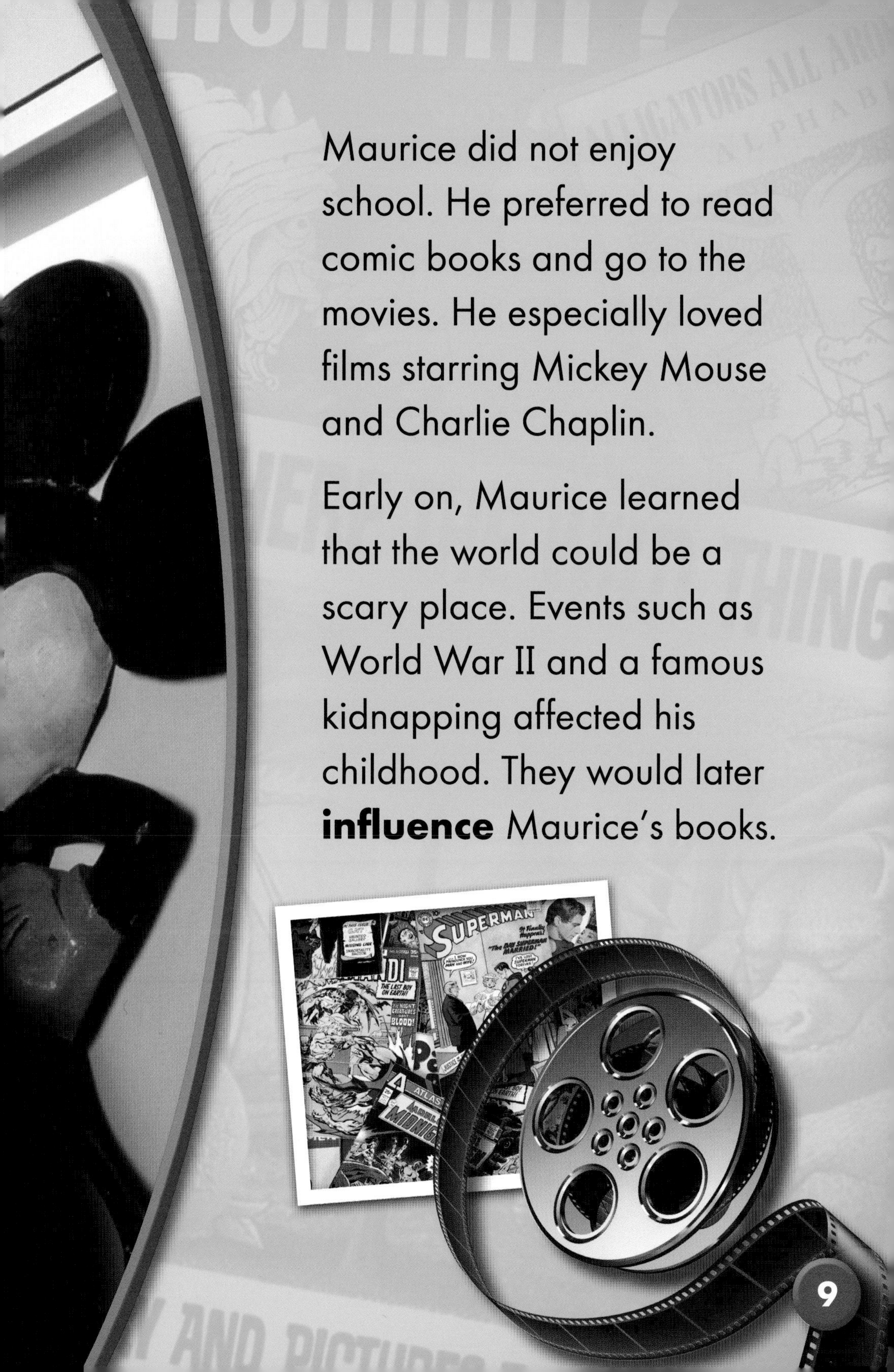

Maurice did not enjoy school. He preferred to read comic books and go to the movies. He especially loved films starring Mickey Mouse and Charlie Chaplin.

Early on, Maurice learned that the world could be a scary place. Events such as World War II and a famous kidnapping affected his childhood. They would later **influence** Maurice's books.

Maurice's Window

In high school, Maurice created cartoons for his school's newspaper. He also had an after-school job drawing backgrounds for comic books.

Maurice illustrated his first book in high school. His teacher wanted fun drawings in the science book he wrote. After he graduated, Maurice continued drawing what he saw out his window. The neighborhood kids **inspired** many later books.

"[A book] arranges itself in your life in a way that is beautiful."
Maurice Sendak

fun fact

Maurice's favorite neighborhood kid was a girl named Rosie. She became the star of his book titled *The Sign on Rosie's Door*.

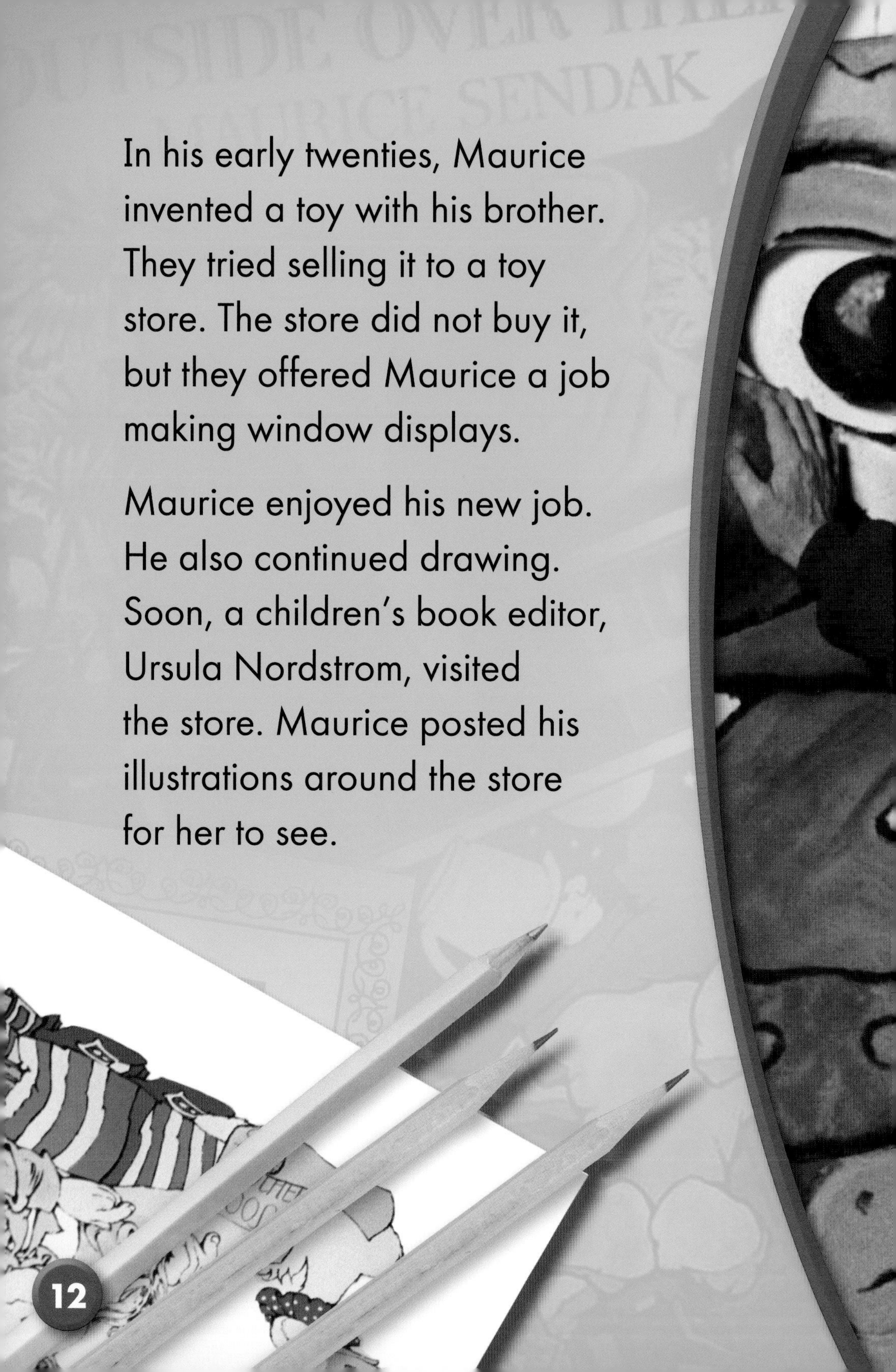

In his early twenties, Maurice invented a toy with his brother. They tried selling it to a toy store. The store did not buy it, but they offered Maurice a job making window displays.

Maurice enjoyed his new job. He also continued drawing. Soon, a children's book editor, Ursula Nordstrom, visited the store. Maurice posted his illustrations around the store for her to see.

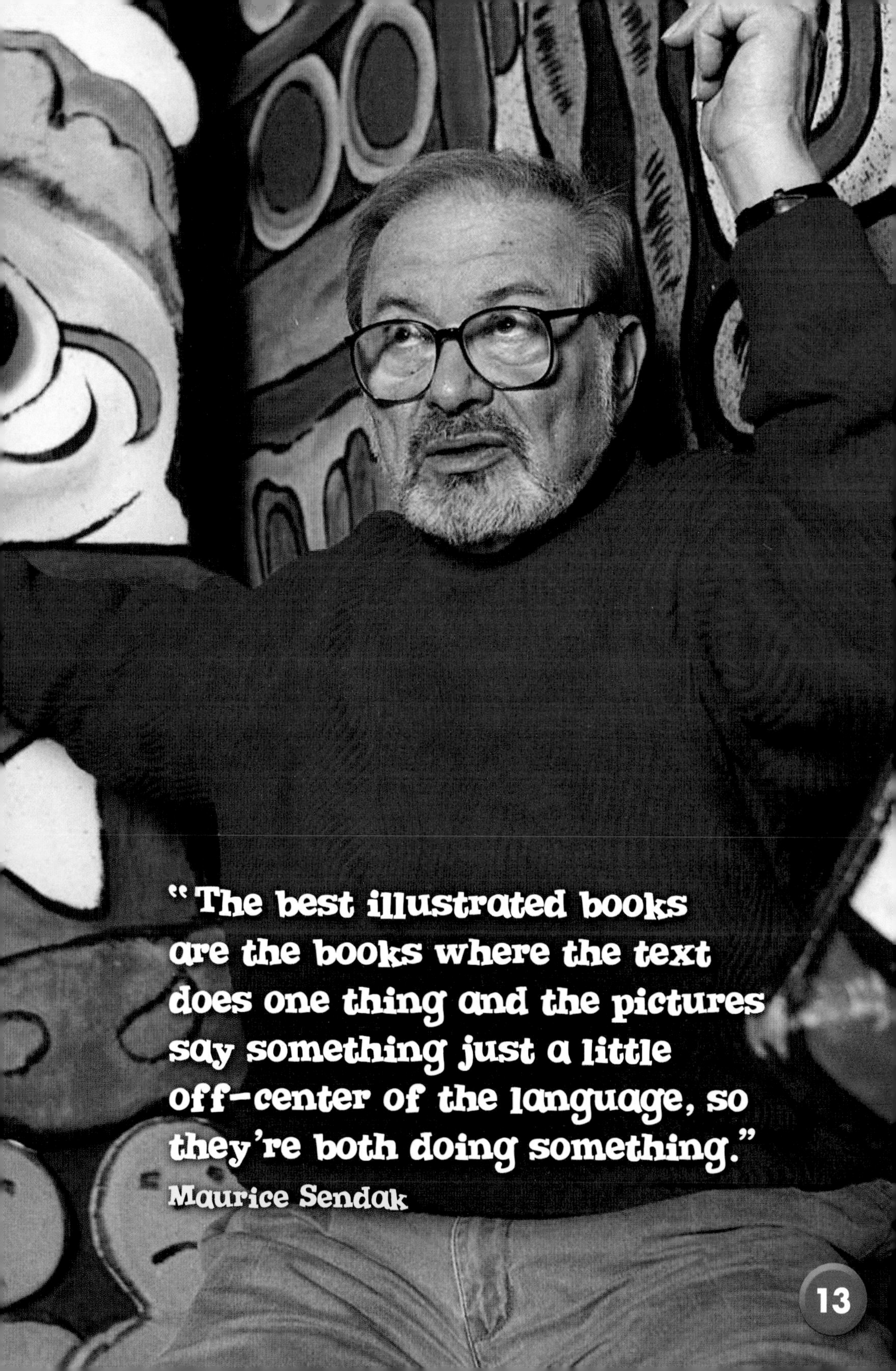

"The best illustrated books are the books where the text does one thing and the pictures say something just a little off-center of the language, so they're both doing something."

Maurice Sendak

The Luck of the Draw

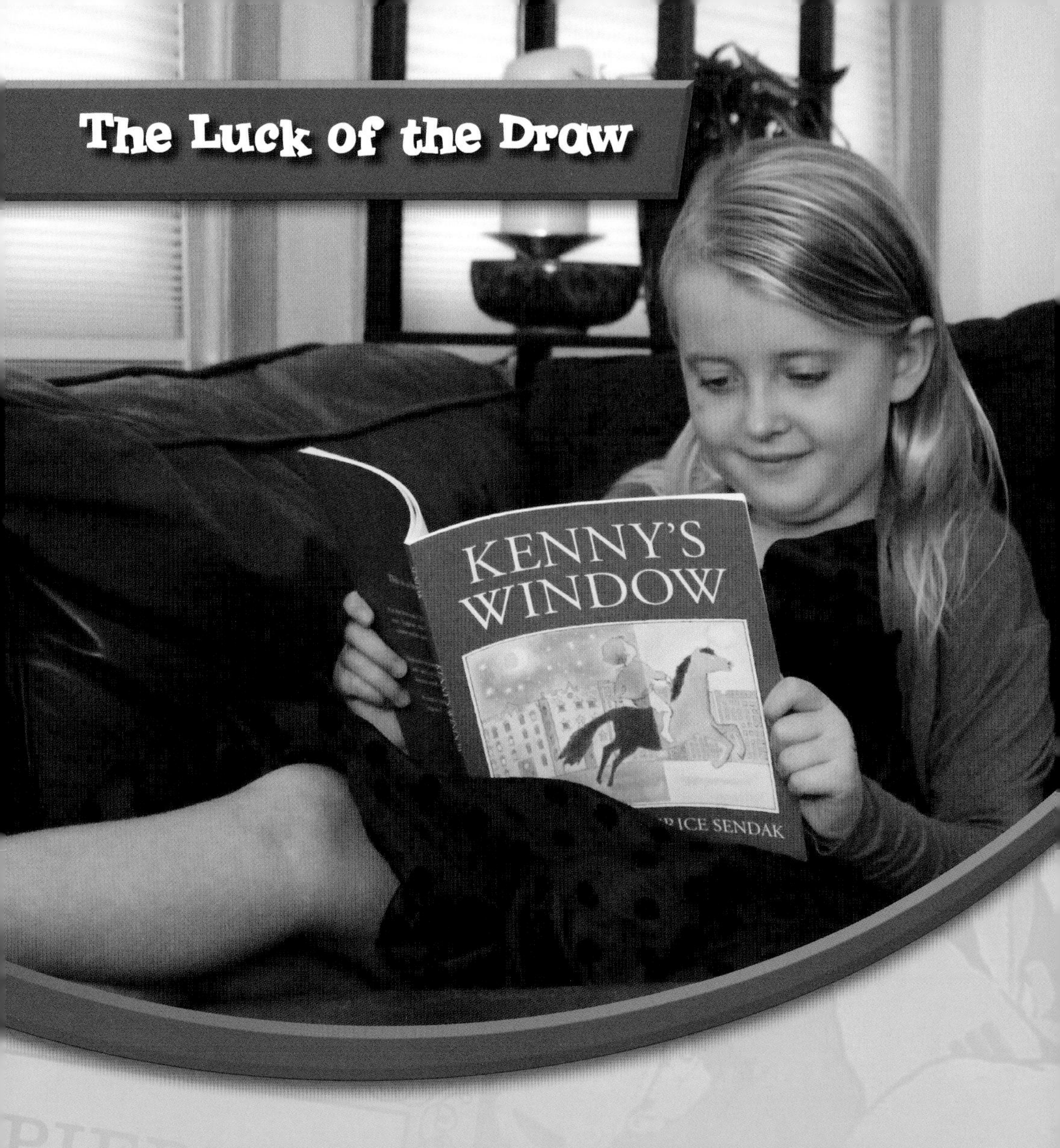

The next day, Ursula asked him to illustrate a book called *The Wonderful Farm.* She continued to give him books to work on. After a few books, he quit his job at the toy store. He became a full-time illustrator!

After illustrating about 20 books, Maurice wrote his own. In 1956, *Kenny's Window* was **published**.

fun fact

Later in life, Maurice spent more than 30 years working on operas. He enjoyed combining his love of music with his love of stories.

Causing a Rumpus

Maurice's books share several **themes**. They often show children in danger. Maurice knew the world can be scary for kids. He did not want to lie in his books.

SELECTED WORKS

Kenny's Window (1956)
Very Far Away (1957)
The Sign on Rosie's Door (1960)
The Nutshell Library (1962)
Where the Wild Things Are (1963)
Higglety Pigglety Pop! Or: There Must Be More to Life (1967)
In the Night Kitchen (1970)
Outside Over There (1981)
Bumble-Ardy (2011)
My Brother's Book (2013)

fun fact

Maurice had a dog named Jennie. She appeared in each book Maurice drew while she was alive.

However, his characters are brave in the face of danger. They stand up to evil in the world. Then they use their imaginations to return to safety.

Maurice's characters are often not nice. They can be mean and bossy. Many do not listen to their parents.

Some adults do not like the characters' bad behavior. Others worry about how scary Maurice's books are. Because of this, many people have tried to **censor** his books.

POP CULTURE CONNECTION

In 2009, *Where the Wild Things Are* came out in theaters. The film used actors and computer effects to bring Max and the wild things to life.

fun fact

Where the Wild Things Are was first called *Where the Wild Horses Are.* Maurice changed the story because he could not draw horses well.

King of All Wild Things

> "If I've done anything, I've had kids express themselves as they are."
> Maurice Sendak

Millions of children have followed Max's journey to the wild things. Many have also enjoyed the dozens of other books Maurice wrote and illustrated during his 60-year **career**.

Maurice passed away on May 8, 2012. But he left behind an amazing number of stories that encourage kids to use their imaginations.

IMPORTANT DATES

1928: Maurice Sendak is born on June 10.

1947: Maurice illustrates *Atomics for the Millions* for his high school science teacher.

1951: *The Wonderful Farm* is the first children's book Maurice illustrates.

1956: Maurice writes his first book, *Kenny's Window*.

1964: *Where the Wild Things Are* wins the Caldecott Medal.

1970: Maurice wins the Hans Christian Andersen Award for illustration.

1983: The American Library Association gives Maurice the Laura Ingalls Wilder Award.

1996: Maurice receives the National Medal of Arts for his life's work in art.

2003: The Astrid Lindgren Memorial Award is awarded to Maurice by the Swedish government for his work in children's literature.

2012: Maurice passes away on May 8.

Glossary

Caldecott Medal—an award given each year to the best-illustrated children's book in America; the Caldecott Medal is given to first place and Caldecott Honors are given to the runners-up.

career—a job someone does for a long time

censor—to remove or change because something is considered dangerous or upsetting

illustrator—an artist who draws pictures for books

influence—to cause something to happen or change

innocent—free from bad experiences in the world

inspired—gave someone an idea about what to do or create

published—printed for a public audience

themes—important ideas or messages

To Learn More

AT THE LIBRARY

Guillain, Charlotte. *Maurice Sendak*. Chicago, Ill.: Heinemann Library, 2012.

Hurtig, Jennifer. *Maurice Sendak*. New York, N.Y.: AV2 by Weigl, 2013.

Sendak, Maurice. *Where the Wild Things Are.* New York, N.Y.: HarperCollins, 1991.

ON THE WEB

Learning more about Maurice Sendak is as easy as 1, 2, 3.

1. Go to www.factsurfer.com.
2. Enter "Maurice Sendak" into the search box.
3. Click the "Surf" button and you will see a list of related web sites.

With factsurfer.com, finding more information is just a click away.

Index

The images in this book are reproduced through the courtesy of: Peter Brooker/ REX/ Newscom, front cover (left); MBR/ KRT/ Newscom, front cover (right); Domini Brown, pp. 4, 11 (top), 16, 17, 19 (top), 21; James Keyser/ Getty Images, pp. 5, 19 (bottom); Kristin Callahan/ Photoshot, p. 7 (top); Africa Studio, p. 7 (bottom); David Corio/ Getty Images, p. 8; ivn3da, p. 9 (top); Wisconsinart, p. 9 (bottom); Associated Press/ AP Images, pp. 11 (bottom), 13; Butterfly Hunter, p. 12 (top left); oksana2010, p. 12 (top right); Ron Galella/ Getty Images, p. 12 (bottom); Emily Porter, p. 14; Glyndebourne Festival Opera/ Ira Nowinski/ Corbis, p. 15; Ronald Grant/ Mary E/ Age Fotostock, p. 18; Spencer Platt/ Getty Images, p. 20.